Bend, Don't Break

Finding Your Inner Strength When Life Gets Rough

Freudian Trips

Copyright Page

Disclaimer

The views and opinions expressed in this book are those of the author(s) and do not necessarily reflect the official policy or position of any other agency, organization, employer, or company. The contents of this book are for informational and educational purposes only and are not intended to serve as professional advice, diagnosis, or treatment.

The information provided in this book is believed to be accurate and reliable as of the date of publication. However, it may include some errors or inaccuracies, and no warranty or guarantee is provided regarding the accuracy, timeliness, or applicability of the content.

Readers are encouraged to consult with professional philosophers, educators, or other qualified professionals where appropriate for personalized advice. The author(s) and publisher shall not be liable for any loss, damage, or harm caused or alleged to be caused, directly or indirectly, by the information or ideas contained, suggested, or referenced in this book.

Chapter 1: When Life Hits Hard

Life can be beautiful, but it can also be brutal. At some point, almost everyone will encounter trauma - a deeply distressing or disturbing experience that overwhelms our ability to cope. Trauma comes in many forms, from surviving a violent assault or natural disaster to living through combat, abuse, or a serious accident. Other traumatic events shake us to the core emotionally, like the loss of a loved one, a heartbreaking betrayal, or chronic childhood neglect.

Trauma is unavoidable; around 70% of adults in the U.S. have endured at least one traumatic event. Some people will experience multiple traumas over their lifetimes. Men, women, and children of all ages and backgrounds suffer trauma. This book is for anyone trying to find their footing after life has knocked them down, no matter what caused their pain or how long ago it occurred.

When trauma strikes, it can feel like we'll never recover. It's easy to get overwhelmed by fear, anger, grief, or shame. Trauma often haunts people for years through upsetting memories, anxiety, numbness, and relationship troubles. Many develop debilitating conditions like post-traumatic stress disorder (PTSD) or addiction. But while trauma leaves indelible scars, the good news is that with care and courage, even after serious hardships, it is possible to heal, grow stronger, and reclaim our lives.

This book explores the profound impacts trauma has on us and how we can cultivate resilience - the ability to "bend" without completely "breaking." Drawing on psychology research, survivor stories, and the author's experience, it offers insight and practical strategies to help work through painful memories, build inner strength, and flourish again after adversity.

While the hurt may never disappear fully, trauma survivors have incredible potential to transform their suffering into meaning, purpose, and service to others. With compassion, community, and the remarkable human capacity for growth, even out of life's darkest moments we can emerge wiser, kinder, and more at peace. If you carry wounds from trauma, know you are not alone. Healing takes time and courage, but it is possible to get your spark back and start feeling whole again. This book will light the way.

Chapter 2: Facing the Damage

Trauma takes endless forms, but the common thread is that it deeply shakes us psychologically and physiologically. Let's examine different types of traumatic experiences and their impacts.

Physical trauma includes surviving acts of violence like assault, rape, domestic abuse, mugging, shootings, and severe accidents. The trauma stems both from the harm done to one's body as well as the sheer terror of life being in peril. Long after physical wounds heal, many survivors grapple with feelings of vulnerability, rage, and injustice. They may relive memories of the attack through nightmares and flashbacks. Some try to numb their distress with alcohol or drugs. The trauma of physical violence shakes us at our core, making it hard to feel safe again.

Emotional trauma can be elusive yet incredibly damaging. It may emerge from ongoing situations like childhood neglect, narcissistic parenting, entrapment in abusive relationships, bullying, or severe gaslighting. The trauma builds slowly over months or years, leaving scars on self-worth. Victims learn to silence their feelings and distrust their inner voice. Healing requires relearning that one's thoughts and emotions matter.

Community-wide traumas stem from historical events like genocide, war, natural disasters, or public violence. Entire groups experience fear, horror, heartbreak, and injustice. The grief becomes woven into collective identity and passed between generations. Healing involves public mourning, social activism, and rebuilding ties.

Here are two hypothetical case studies illustrating trauma's impacts:

Mia survived an abusive relationship that eroded her self-esteem for years. Her ex often berated and belittled her in private, convincing Mia the put-downs were "just jokes." In public he was charming, depriving Mia of allies. She repressed her own emotions to avoid his anger. Even after leaving him, Mia struggles with depression, distrusts her feelings, and avoids intimacy. She often feels corrupted and unlovable. Recovery has required acknowledging the abuse was real and rebuilding her worth.

Patrick witnessed combat at 19 that haunts him still today. Now loud noises make him panic, as if under attack. He suffers recurrent nightmares where his comrades die while he stands paralyzed. Patrick tries to avoid anything triggering memories, but feels detached and on edge. He drinks to numb his anxiety. Recovery involves processing grief, re-establishing connections, and confronting once-terrifying reminders that he survived and is safe now in the present.

Healing from trauma is challenging work. But by facing our wounds with compassion, we can finally start feeling whole again. The next chapter delves into the thorny impacts of complex trauma.

Chapter 3: The Damage That Lingers

Single incidents of trauma can scar people emotionally. But recurring, relentless trauma often inflicts even deeper harm with lasting impacts on mental health. This "complex trauma" emerges from sustained experiences like childhood abuse or neglect, domestic violence, human trafficking, and extended combat. Let's explore why complex trauma wounds cut so deeply and how to foster healing.

By definition, complex trauma happens repeatedly and cumulatively, often when people are powerless to escape. Examples include growing up with a volatile alcoholic parent or enduring months as a prisoner of war. The traumas layer upon each other, creating a climate of constant anxiety and fear. Victims carry no safe haven from the terror.

Over time, chronic stress from trauma chemically alters the brain, leading to changes like:

- Heightened activity in fear-response regions, making threats feel exaggerated

- Reduced functioning of decision-making areas, hindering planning and logic

- Disruption of neurotransmitters that regulate mood, increasing depression/anxiety

- Weakened ability to self-regulate emotions, causing outbursts and numbness

For survivors, past trauma feels ever-present. Painful memories intrude uncontrollably. Many develop PTSD and other mental health issues like addiction, eating disorders, and suicidal thinking. Ongoing nightmares, panic attacks, and flashbacks of being trapped make it hard for survivors to feel calm or safe.

Complex trauma also corrodes one's sense of identity and self-worth. Victims internalize the violence or neglect as their own fault, feeling defective to their core. Lasting impacts may include:

- Profound distrust and social withdrawal

- Feeling constantly on guard or under attack

- Difficulty identifying and expressing emotions

- Loss of personal empowerment and agency

Healing requires professional help and time to grieve, process memories, rebuild inner security, and reconnect to others. Power returns by reclaiming one's autonomy, values, and strengths. Yet while complex trauma casts a heavy shadow, with courage and support we can find light again. There is always hope.

Chapter 4: Developing Your Bounce-Back Power

Resilience is the ability to adapt and rebound after adversity. Trauma survivors especially need resilience to process painful events, regain stability, and heal. The good news is resilience thrives from certain mindsets and actions we can cultivate. Let's explore strategies to boost resilience on the journey to recovery.

Protective factors that foster resilience include:

- Social support - Connecting with others who listen, care, and affirm your worth. Support groups can be invaluable.

- Finding purpose - Discovering meaningful goals and causes beyond yourself.

- Embracing growth - Viewing recovery as a journey of wisdom-gaining and self-discovery.

- Self-care - Attending to your needs for rest, healthy food, stress management, and physical activity.

- Sense of control - Believing you can influence outcomes through your choices.

- Optimism - Maintaining hope and viewing setbacks as temporary obstacles to overcome.

When trauma triggers overwhelming emotions, try grounding techniques like:

- Slow deep breathing

- Noting sensory details (smells, textures, colors) in your environment

- Stating truths, like "I am safe now"

- Imagining your distress flowing out as you exhale

- Listening to soothing music or inspirational messages

- Exercising, stretching, or meditation

For long-term resilience, be vigilant of negative self-talk that fuels shame. Counter attacks on your worth with affirmations like "This pain is not my fault" and "I deserve to heal." Seek to reframe trauma not as a failing, but an experience to learn from about your strength.

While the struggle continues, know that you can build your resilience muscle over time. Each small act of courage, self-care, and hope lights the path forward.

Chapter 5: Rising Up

Trauma tries to dim our light. Yet remarkably, many survivors eventually flourish again, not just despite their pain but because of it. Their wounds open the door to profound growth.

While trauma always leaves scars, in its wake we can discover newfound strength, purpose, and wisdom. This "post-traumatic growth" emerges as we process trauma and make meaning from suffering. The journey is gradual, uneven, and ongoing. But here are some growth experiences trauma survivors often report:

- **Increased resilience and self-reliance**

- **Deeper bonds with others who suffered**

- **Greater compassion and urgency to help others**

- **Refocused values like living with more presence**

- **Renewed faith in one's own perseverance**

- Desire to advocate for causes like justice, peace, and healing

Consider activists like Phyllis Hyman, who transformed family tragedy into Mothers Against Drunk Driving. Or Henri Nouwen, who ministered with humility to others' wounds after his own mental health crisis. At times the difference between being debilitated by trauma and finding growth is the ability to turn pain into shared purpose.

Yet while post-traumatic growth is real, toxic positivity hinders healing. Prodded to "get over it" or "see the silver lining," survivors feel guilt and shame. Recovery is a mourning process. We must give ourselves permission to grieve what was lost before discovering what was gained. With time and care, we can emerge wiser - not just restored to who we were, but open to who we can become. Scars remain, but do not define us.

The path winds on. Trust that light waits ahead.

Chapter 6: When Trauma Gets Learned and Passed Down

Healing from trauma begins by recognizing it doesn't happen in a vacuum. Traumatic events often stem from societal forces of injustice, fear, and scarcity. Poverty, oppression, and bigotry breed trauma. To reduce suffering, our communities must do better at nurturing all people.

Consider the epidemic of urban youth gun violence. The trauma multiplies with each new shooting, as teens nationwide are hypervigilant for impending attack. Many expect they'll die young and see violence as unavoidable - symptoms of post-traumatic stress. They carry generations of pain from living in communities destabilized by systemic racism, disinvestment, and mass incarceration.

Or look at the traumatic impact on LGBTQ youth from being bullied and rejected for their identity. Many internalize society's messages that they are sinful, abnormal, even unworthy of life. The wounds drive high rates of depression, anxiety, and suicide. Supportive communities could help prevent so much pain.

Intergenerational cycles of abuse and addiction also breed trauma. Children witnessing or enduring neglect and violence are at grave risk to perpetuate it later in life. Only by fostering secure families and childhoods free from terror can we break the vicious cycle.

Clearly trauma will continue intruding, even into lives that seem pristine on the surface, until we remedy crises like poverty, bigotry, exploitation, and addiction corroding communities. By listening to those who suffer, looking within at our own pain, and addressing these issues at their root, perhaps someday trauma will be far less common.

But for now, we must keep shining light wherever darkness lingers, extending hands to those who are hurting, speaking up against injustice, and working to prevent trauma so that all people can feel safe, valued, and free to thrive.

Chapter 7: Where To Go From Here

Healing from trauma is a lifelong journey. The wounds may never fully disappear. You will carry memories of loss, flashes of fear, and lingering sadness. Yet while the past remains part of you, with courage you can keep moving forward. Here are some closing reflections:

The work of recovery continues, even once the most intense pain subsides. Be patient and caring with yourself. Healing isn't linear. There will still be hard days when trauma echoes. Build resilience by reaching out for support on the difficult days, practicing self-care, and refocusing on the present.

But also make space to honor your journey. Share your experiences with others to lighten their load. Seek meaning in the pain. Allow yourself to fully feel both the sorrow and the strength that adversity awakened in you. Find opportunities to offer yourself the compassion and safety you needed back then.

Trauma can teach us powerful lessons about human resilience, love, and what matters most. Your pain matters, but does not have to overshadow the gifts and purpose that exist beyond it. Healing means reclaiming your whole self - the broken parts, the healed parts, and everything in between. Be gentle yet brave enough to keep becoming the person life interrupted.

Wherever you are on this journey, please know you don't walk alone. Others have been here too, and we still stand with you. By sharing our stories, we light the way for each other and for those who will follow after, through fear and heartbreak into wisdom, purpose, and peace. Keep going, dear one. There is so much love and life ahead.

Glossary of Terms

Complex trauma - Repeated and prolonged traumatic experiences, often occurring when someone lacks the ability to escape. Results in deeper psychological and emotional damage.

Hypervigilance - Heightened state of sensory sensitivity and alertness for potential threats. Common in trauma survivors as part of a chronically activated nervous system.

Post-traumatic growth - Positive psychological changes that can result from struggling to overcome trauma and its aftermath. Can include increased perspective, meaning, personal strength, gratitude, optimism, etc.

Post-traumatic stress disorder (PTSD) - Psychological disorder resulting from traumatic exposure. Symptoms include intrusive memories, hypervigilance, emotional numbing, etc. Caused by a protective nervous system stuck in overdrive.

Resilience - Capacity to adapt and recover in the face of adversity. Ability to "bounce back" and grow stronger when faced with trauma and stress.

Self-compassion - Treating oneself with care, concern and kindness - especially during struggle or failure. Lowers stress hormones. Promotes resilience.

Self-efficacy - Belief in one's capability to influence events and overcome challenges. Key component of resilience.

Social support - Close relationships that provide ongoing care, affection, belonging and assistance. Critical for trauma recovery and resilience.

Toxic positivity - Promoting positive thinking to an extreme degree. Shutting down negative emotions and grief by insisting on highlighting optimistic perspectives. Can hinder trauma processing.

Triggers - Experiences (sensory impressions, situations, emotions, etc) that suddenly recall memories of past trauma and renew associated psychological/emotional distress.

Vicarious trauma - Indirect trauma exposure from caring for others who have experienced trauma. Can affect helpers like therapists, first responders, nurses.

About Freudian Trips

Welcome to Freudian Trips, your dedicated platform for diving deep into the world of psychology. We are more than just a YouTube channel or a book publisher. We are a beacon of enlightenment, making complex psychological concepts accessible and engaging for all.

Our YouTube channel is a rich repository of psychology made simple. We take the profound and often complex ideas from the world of psychology and break them down into digestible, easy-to-understand content. From the foundational theories of Freud to the cognitive insights of Piaget, we cover a broad spectrum of psychological schools and thoughts, making psychology accessible to everyone, regardless of their background or prior knowledge.

As a book publisher, we take the same approach, transforming intricate psychological theories into comprehensible narratives. Our books are not just collections of words, but vessels of wisdom that make psychology approachable and relatable. We believe that psychology should not be confined to academic circles, but should be available to all who seek to understand the human mind and behavior.

At Freudian Trips, we believe in the power of curiosity and the pursuit of knowledge. We are here to stoke the fires of your curiosity, to guide you on your intellectual journey, and to help you navigate the fascinating world of psychology.

If you are someone who is not afraid to question, to explore, and to learn, then you are in the right place. Join us on this journey of exploration, as we make psychology easy to understand, one concept at a time.

Be sure to visit our Youtube channel at: www.freudiantrips.com/youtube

You can also visit us on the web at www.freudiantrips.com

Welcome to The Freudian Trip community. Stay curious. Stay enlightened.